Spiritually Decalcify the Pineal Gland

Rebecca Marina Messenger

Table of Contents

Dedication

Dedicated to All the Divine Ladies who constantly surround me...and to my Mortal precious Friend Cindy Cook.

Cindy,

You are such a treasure.

You have a heart of gold, a spirit so sweet, a mind swift to find solutions, the willingness to always be of help with your immeasurable talents.

...and you're doggone fun to hang out with!

The world is blessed by your presence.

About the Author

After a powerful visit from Archangel Gabriel, Rebecca's life changed forever!

Rebecca became committed to encouraging others to "call on the angels."

Because the Divine Visit enhanced her Psychic abilities, Rebecca easily "Tunes in" to the Spirit world. She teaches classes worldwide via the internet that help others to advance spiritually and awaken their own latent abilities.

Rebecca is the mother of five wonderful children and 3 grandchildren. Spending time with them is one of her greatest joys. Her favorite hobby is dancing…and you can find Rebecca joyfully expressing the Divine on the dance floor regularly!

This is a channeled text. It is not meant to diagnose, prescribe, or cure any disease or to serve as a substitute for medical advice.

Author's Note

I cannot take credit for any of the Wonderful, Healing Information I receive.

I do take credit for Showing up, Trusting, and saying 'YES' to the Divine Guidance that is always there. And yes, sometimes it sounds just a wee bit Crazy ...until I pass it through the Never-Fail filter of my heart.

Take what resonates with you and leave the rest.

Love,

Rebecca Marina Messenger
October 19, 2014

Spiritually Decalcify the Pineal Gland

Presented by: Rebecca Marina Messenger (and Spirit Friends)

Transcribed from a live session in April 2014

In order to keep the integrity of the original transmission - this is presented in conversational style as much as possible. That is not always in keeping with perfect grammatical style.

To get Your FREE Audio version of this Method, visit http://wp.me/Pq2xG — 2FR.

This is a brief explanation, followed by a longer meditation that does the work for you.

Rebecca: So, while we're waiting, just ask your angels and guides to help you to get the very most out of this.

This is Rebecca Marina Messenger, and I'm so happy today, because this is my birthday, and the very best gift I could give you is to help you to decalcify your pineal gland.

It's come to my awareness that this gland is, of course, very important as a spiritual healer; we all know that. And as a spiritual follower, you probably know that, and just with age, the pineal starts to calcify. Fluoride is the really big enemy, you might say, of the pineal gland: the lifestyle, the white flour, the white sugar. All of these add to calcification.

What a lot of folks don't know, and I discovered in my research, is that there is fluid inside the pineal gland, and yes, it calcifies some on the outside; but the real damage comes from the inside — the fluid is not free to move around.

There are actually rods and cones inside your pineal gland, much like the retina of an eye. So, it really is a third eye, and the fluid is to bathe and enhance — everything is more vivid in water.

Sound is four times more effective in water and if you've ever noticed, when you're taking a shower or you get in a bath, you often get divine guidance or a great inspiration. So, in today's message, we're going to be assisted by all kind of angels, light beings, and…the animal kingdom. So how the heck is this going to happen?

I'm going to guide you. I do ask that you <u>don't</u> drive a vehicle while listening to this, and afterwards, <u>please</u> don't sign any divorce papers or very important documents, because we will be going deep into the mid-brain. So I'd like to say thank you to my own spiritual team.

My guru in the astral plane, Sri Yukteswar, who was the guru of Yogananda, very dear to my heart. Dr Pillai or Babaji, as he's called, who is my guru teacher in the flesh. You can check out his work at www.pillaicenter.com.

I give him so much credit for some of this mid-brain knowledge that I'm going to be sharing with you.

I want to thank all my angels, all the guides, all the ascended masters, the god and goddesses of all our ancestors who are here. Oh, someone's popping up. **There's some of your animal pets that have crossed over that want you to know that they're right here with you and they're so excited, because guess what?** When you do this clearing, you're going to be able to communicate better with animal spirits that are departed as well.

So, I'd also like to say thank you to Anwar, my friend from Atlantis, who gave me a chant that you can use now, and I'm going to give you a quickie version to use on a daily basis, and I want to thank Isis for her wisdom.

A while back, Isis gave me a technique which I'm not going to share the whole thing today. I'm just going to tell you about it. The pineal gland is directly associated with the sexual organs: the clitoris of a woman, the head of a penis of a man. You talk about having some hot sex, baby.

Hook up the pineal with your sexual organs. That's another class. I'll be announcing that, when that's ready.

So, the pineal gland or the third eye is your gateway to Spirit; however, I was told in this session, "Rebecca, you can't just balance and activate the pineal. It's a gland. There's seven glandular systems. You must also give the treatment to those glands. The pineal is the very highest gland."

11

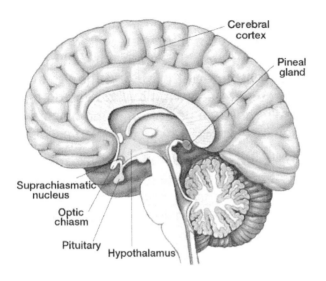

Cerebral cortex

Pineal gland

Suprachiasmatic nucleus

Optic chiasm

Pituitary

Hypothalamus

If you could think of it as the apex, and then all the glands down below will be affected, but we're actually going to do some balancing cleansing of them. So I've made a few notes here I'm reading, because I want to make sure I don't miss anything. I'm just so excited that you're reading this, because I want to hear some stories, how you're tuning in, with your newly awakened and squeaky clean pineal gland. (You can email Rebecca at Rebecca@RebeccaMarina.com.)

So, I want to talk a little bit about the mid-brain, because the mid-brain is more than just the pineal gland. The mid-brain is the thalamus, the pituitary, and the brain stem. So we're going to be working with all of those in the mid-brain.

Now, according to Dr. Pillai and my spiritual guidance, the mid-brain is that part of the brain that used to be considered reptilian. I feel it's a little insulting to be calling our miracle working brain reptilian, but this is the part of the brain that does not know the difference between what might be a material reality and what might be a fantasy reality.

At the end of this, I'm going to guide you into creating your first miracle, and we're just going to bring that miracle that you want, into your mid-brain, bathe it with love, and it will materialize. Since I've been doing these exercises, my life has improved so much.

One thing I'm so happy about the pineal is that since I've been on a spiritual path for years, I've had trouble sleeping. You would think I'd sleep like a baby, but I get ideas. I get guidance. Spirits pop up in my room sometimes.

So, since I've been doing these exercises to decalcify my own pineal, I have been sleeping so much better and waking up refreshed, feeling like a million dollars. That's what I want for you too.

So, let us begin with… just close your eyes and send a wave of gratitude out to the universe, to your angels, to your guides. And, Beloveds, I want you to actually ask your angels and guides for their assistance in this clearing.

You know, we all have angels and guides around us all the time, and their hands are tied, until we ask for help. You might say, well, I asked for help yesterday. Well, ask for help today. Ask for help right now.

So, we want to make sure our pineals are communicating with all the glands and that all our body parts are working better. With closed eyes, having asked your angels and guides for help, I'd like to begin with an exercise. This will begin the meditation. So, if you need to take a drink of water, take it now.

Please honor the process that was given to me, by giving this your full attention, for Beloved, I'm giving you mine. The angels and guides are giving you theirs, and this process is so precious. I honor my guru, Sri Yukteswar, for this exercise called the **unity breath.**

Let us imagine that we're all breathing in together; and even though we're all over the world, we're breathing as one heart, for Beloved, we are indeed of the soul family.

The same soul family that came here to experience life together and Beloved, it is our express intent to bless you, to bless not only your pineal gland, but all the glands and organs within your body to cleanse your aura. And, Beloved, to guide you in the process of creating your own miracles, for this is indeed the golden age that we are entering. This is the time for humanity to begin to realize the spiritual authority that they <u>own</u>, that they were given, and it's time to own that.

Think of a place in nature that you adore. Imagine your favorite place in nature and put yourself there. Imagine that you're barefoot and feel that feeling of the earth beneath your feet. Maybe you're at a beach, and it's sand you're feeling. Maybe you're in a meadow, and it's grass you're feeling.

Maybe you're on a rocky mountain, and it's rock you are feeling beneath your feet. Whatever it is,

Beloved, feel that with the bare bottoms of your feet. Smell the air. And think of the love you have for Mother Earth. And when your heart is filled with love, Beloved, send down a shaft of love to the heart of Earth Mother, to Gaia saying, "Thank you Earth Mother."

Beloveds, Earth Mother is in travail right now. She is birthing many new creations, and what gives her relief from her travail is the appreciation and love of humanity.

And she receives that love and appreciation, and she sends a wave of love back up to you, and you feel it in your heart. Take a deep breath in, breathing that love.

And still feeling that love from divine mother, think of the Milky Way, the Cosmos, and the darkness of the void. Feel the love for Father Sky.

When you have that feeling of overwhelming love, send that love up to the planets, up to the solar systems, up to the universes. For Beloved, you are a child of the universe.

And now, allow yourself to just feel the divine child that you are, feeling yourself wrapped in the love of Mother Earth Father Sky.

Now in the Sufi tradition, the chakras correspond to the glandular system. So, let us put our awareness on the first and second chakras. That would be the root chakra.

And then the next one, which is the sexual chakra, which relates to your survival instincts, your sexuality, and your creativity. The glands are the gonads or the ovaries, depending on male or female.

And then I will be chanting, and you chant after me. As we bring in to the first and second chakra, the light of a thousand suns, the light of Ra. Repeat after me, "Ra.... Ra.... Ra.... Ra.... Ra.... Ra," and feel those two chakras and the corresponding glands filled with the healing light of the sun.

Feel it almost burning with the glorious feeling within you. As the chakras and the glands become synchronized, organized, awakened. Now any healing that needs to be done, is best done in the darkness of the void. And so as the chakra becomes blazing light, receiving the healing of the sun, let it <u>now</u> go into rest.

Imagine the great darkness of the void, pulling the blanket over these two chakras and saying, "Shh. Time to sleep and time to heal…. Time to sleep and time to heal." Be in the silence of respect in this resting time.

And as these two chakras sleep… don't worry, we shall awaken them. For it is our intention that this healing shall begin happening instantly, and we are masters of spiritual authority and if we say it, <u>then it is so</u>.

Bring your awareness <u>now</u> to the third chakra. The solar plexus chakra which corresponds with the adrenal glands. Once more, bringing in the light of a thousand suns, Ra is the name of the sun god. Repeat after me, focusing on the third chakra and your adrenals. "Ra.... Ra.... Ra.... Ra.... Ra.... Ra", the light of a thousand suns beams into your third chakra and the adrenals, lighting it up, burning away any impurities.

Now in the healing silence, we close the door, and the darkness of the great void descends. And pulls a blanket of loving, sweet, enveloping darkness, so that this chakra may rest and continue the healing process.

Move your awareness to the fourth chakra, which is the heart. Oh, Beloveds, I love you so much. Spirit loves you so much. You are so loved. You don't know who you are. You are so loved.

And repeat after me, bringing in the light of a thousand suns, "Ra.... Ra.... Ra.... Ra.... Ra.... Ra.... Ra", your heart is blazing with love, blazing with the healing solar light. The inner sun within you begins to glow, and your heart is filled to overflowing with love for all of humanity. For Mother Earth, Father Sky, for all the kingdoms: the plants, the minerals, the animals, the creatures of the sea.

And now, close the door, and let your heart rest, pulling up that warm, soft, enveloping blanket of darkness, healing darkness of the great void. All is silent, as your heart rests and recovers from so many wounds, Beloved.

Move your awareness to the fifth chakra, the throat, which represents both the thyroid gland and the thymus. The thymus is the greatest organ of immunity that you have within your entire system. So — putting your awareness there, breathe into the throat chakra the light of a thousand suns.

Especially, you light workers who have not been able to speak your truth because of old fears of what people might think.

Breathe in this healing light of the sun and repeat after me. "Ra.... Ra.... Ra.... Ra.... Ra.... Ra.... Ra", and let your throat blaze with the light of a thousand suns. Feel your throat ex-pand-ing.

Feel your voice becoming stronger, as you find the courage to speak out, "I know who I am and I know why I'm here, I'm here to serve, here to love, and I'm here to discover how to put miracles in my life."

Be with that thought as you allow that blanket of soft, soothing, healing darkness, the darkness of the void to just slowly envelop your throat chakra, just for a moment. For moments of healing and resting and we command all of these chakras that we have touched now to continue the healing process.

With your awareness on the pituitary and the hypothalamus, just breathe this light into the pituitary and the hypothalamus. "Ra.... Ra.... Ra.... Ra.... Ra.... Ra.... Ra." Just allow the light of a thousand suns to blaze through your pituitary and hypothalamus.

And now let that sweet, kind, darkness envelop, and let the healing begin in the resting period. And now straight into the pineal gland, breathe the light of Ra. "Ra.... Ra.... Ra.... Ra.... Ra.... Ra.... Ra.... Ra."

The light of a thousand suns fills your pineal gland with light. Beginning even now, the decalcification process, stirring the waters within your pineal. Heal thyself…. heal thyself…. heal thyself. Soul of my pineal gland, heal thyself. Angels, assist.

And then allow that envelope of darkness just to temporarily sleep…. sleep…. sleep. Now your whole system is in a state of rest and healing…. rest and healing. Allow it to be easy…. allow it to be easy.

In a few moments, we will begin to reawaken all of these systems after their rest, but now, let us move to the actual brain, let us fill the entire brain with light. And if the pineal wakes up, so be it. It can take the rest it needs in an instant, for the pineal is part of the astral plane and in the astral plane, when you ask for something, it is instantly delivered.

Pay attention, I'm going to say that again. The pineal gland is the gateway to the astral plane, part of the astral plane.

Learning to honor this and knowing that what you can command, can become true. **When you ask for something in the astral plane, there is no waiting.**

Put your focus on your right eye, and receive a beam of light into your right eye. Focusing on that intense beam of light, cross it over to the left side of the brain.

By the way, if you begin to feel any little roaring sounds or pops or clicks, it's simply your brain healing — be not alarmed. Receive a beam of light into the left eye and cross the beam of light over to the right brain. Now just have your awareness on both eyes being filled with light.

Receive a beam of light into the third eye, straight back to the pineal and to the brain stem. Stimulation…. Receive a beam of light into the right nostril, breathe it in. It fills your sinus cavities with light. Receive a beam of light into the left nostril. Breathe that light in. It fills your sinus cavities with light.

Receive a beam of light into the right ear. It activates all the tiny little hairs within your eardrum system. Receive a beam of light into your left ear, it activates all the tiny little hairs in your eardrum system. Your whole head is now beaming with the light of a thousand suns.

The light travels up to the corpus callosum, and then is distributed throughout the neocortex in a healthy manner. Your mid-brain is active, filled with light, ready to ascend into the astral plane.

Ask your angels for assistance with any sensations you may be feeling. Now we have our chakras and glands in alignment. Chakras still sleeping…. Mid-brain is filled with light.

Let us begin the bathing of the spinal column fluid. This is the long version to do this. There will be a shorty quickie, but you must do this one first.

Place your awareness on the base of the spine. Place your awareness on the spinal column fluid within the spine. Beginning at the base of the spine, receive the element of fire into the base of your spine and into that spinal column fluid.

Receive the element of fire, call it to you, and it must come!

Honor the element of fire. The fire that gave that life. **The fire within yourself.** The fire that you cannot live without, Beloveds.

Call the element of the earth and all the carbon-based creatures into your spinal column fluid. And when you say, **"Earth element, come to me," it must obey.** And you honor that earth element and you receive it into the composition of your spinal column fluid.

Call the element of water. Element of water, be present fully in my spinal column fluid, purify now! I honor you, element of water.

And now element of spirit, Om, come into my spinal column fluid. Fill me with the spirit of all of creation. Fill me with light.

Putting your awareness on your spinal column fluid. My soul shall speak to your soul. As this fluid is here, let us receive the sacred language that is the language of the heart. Each one having his own sacred language, I shall share mine with you. Into the spinal column fluid, I give you this gift of sacred language, light language from my soul to your soul.

Having your awareness there, the fluid is eager to receive this gift of love. *[chanting sacred soul language 00:29:16 — 00:29:28] Feel the reverberations throughout all your spinal column fluid. I give you this gift of love from deep within my heart, deep within my soul. *[chanting 00:29:40 — 00:30:13] An-Nūr…. An-Nūr…. An-

Nūr. (Pronounced Ahn Noor) And now your spinal column fluid is filled with all of the sacred elements, and it's filled with the gift of love from my soul to you.

The fluid begins to ascend. The light from this fluid wakes up the sleeping chakras. Wake from your sleep, first chakra. Wake and receive this gift of spinal column fluid filled with light, love, and all the powers of the elements — awake, refreshed. Moving slowly upward to the second chakra, awake, refreshed.

Moving slowly and caressing the third chakra. Receive the nutrients of love, of the elements, and awake, refreshed. Moving up to the throat chakra, to the heart chakra. Receive the elements, receive the love. Moving to the throat chakra.

Receiving the elements, receiving the love. Moving to the third eye chakra. Receiving the elements, receiving the love. Moving to the crown, receive the elements, receive the love. Now the fluid descends again and it caresses each of your glands and chakras until you feel this deliciousness, sensuality, almost sexual.

The fluid ascends again and descends caressing all of the nerve endings in your body attached to the spinal column, caressing each and every chakra, leaving you in a state of ecstasy.

And now the spinal column fluid ascends once more and begins to bathe the tissues. And don't worry, there's plenty of spinal column fluid. You will not run out. There is no scarcity in the astral plane, Beloved.

Command it, and it is so.

The spinal column fluid begins to caress and bathe the brain stem, and it just ever so slowly begins to fill the entire mid-brain cavity. And as this process is very slowly happening, we're going to create divine rain to cleanse your outer aura, to cleanse your skin, and then to open the crown and begin to bathe from above, so below… so above.

Spinal column fluid, coming upward into the mid-brain. Divine rain, moving downward into the mid-brain, creating miracles.

Put your awareness on the higher self-point. This is 18 to 24 inches above your head. Ask for help with this. Ask all your angels, all your guides, to begin together in your higher self-point. It can be as large as you desire.

Invite all the gods and goddesses, your ancestors, to gather, to create this divine healing elixir. Ask for it, and it shall be so. Ask for this divine elixir, this divine rain to be created for your benefit.

And breathe in love. Be that gratitude to all these divine beings who willingly, lovingly help you.

Breathe out that gratitude, breath in that love. Feel the amount of the elixir beginning to build …and to build …and to build. Now you extend your hand and receive the divine rain. As the rain begins to descend upon you, cleansing your auric field, cleansing your skin.

You dance like a little kid in the ecstasy of the divine rain. The divine rain makes you sing praises from your heart. And as you sing praises from your heart, the beings of light receive your praise, receive your honor, and even increase the flow of divine healing rain.

If there is any place in your body that is hurting now, direct this rain to go there, now. And allow yourself to thirstily drink it in.

Now, imagine that the very crown of your head is opening, and the divine rain pours through the corpus callosum, through all the neocortex and into the entire mid-brain system.

Bathing the pineal lovingly, as a mother would bath her baby child. Bathing the brain stem, the thalamus, the pituitary. Now the entire cavity is filled with divine rain and the essence of all the elements from your spinal column fluid.

Be in the space of enjoying this divine rain, this divine element. The mixture of the divine rain and the power of your spinal column fluid, which has its own consciousness, causes a vibration to begin within your mid-brain that is already beginning the decalcification process, both inside and outside your pineal. Not only that, but the thalamus, the pituitary, the brain stem, all that has collected particles of sediment, begin to be healed.

And now, because sound is four times more effective in water, and we have filled the mid-brain and bathed the entire brain with holy divine rain and holy divine spinal column fluid, we begin the chant from Atlantis given to me by Anwar, chief medical officer of Atlantis, who indeed exists within the astral plane.

And if you would like his assistance personally, simply ask him, "Anwar, will you assist me?" The chant is a simple one; it's Nome, N – O – M – E. I chant it and you chant it after me, allowing the vibrations of this sound to begin to <u>further</u> cleanse the entire mid-brain area.

"Nome…. Nome…. Nome…. Nome….. Nome…. Nome…. Nome…. Nome." The sound of thousands of people is going out throughout all the world, affecting not only <u>our</u> mid-brains and pineals, but <u>others</u> who are ready in their hearts to receive this healing.

Let us continue. "Nome…. Nome…. Nome…. Nome….. Nome…. Nome…. Nommmmmme…. Nommmmmme." Feel the vibration as you close your lips on the M sound. Nommmmmmmmmmmmmme.

Feel the loosening power as you begin with the N sound. Nnnnnnnnn, like a jackhammer, Nnnnnnnnommmmmmme…. Nnnnnnnnommmmmmme….. Nnnnnnnnommmmmmme….. Nnnnnnnnommmmmmme….. Nnnnnnnnommmmmmme….. Nnnnnnnnommmmmmme….. Nnnnnnnnommmmmmme….. Be in the silence; be in the silence.

Now we shall receive some unexpected assistance from the animal kingdom. Make the opening of your third eye larger. You are now in the astral plane and you can command and create anything that you desire. Own it.

And your third eye is larger. Invite three whales. Whales… they are my friends. Enter three beautiful whales. Benjamin, the guardian of the deep. His mate Sarai, their offspring Samuel.

Invite them in… send them love. They are here to assist you. It's important to invite them in, and they acclimate themselves to your mid-brain area. And this is now the astral plane, you may create whatever you desire. Send them love, and ask for their assistance.

In decalcifying your pineal, how can they assist you? … Because they have sonar. They have eco location. They are able to send out pulsations that will dislodge inside and outside, and since you are in water, it will effortlessly be carried away, be dissolved. Have you asked them?

Repeat after me. "Dear friends, please use your sonar to loosen the calcifications that have me bound." I will repeat, and you repeat after me. "Dear friends, please use your sonar to loosen the calcifications that have me bound."

Be in the mode of receiving, for they are here to serve. Not all light workers are human. Many, many light workers are in the animal kingdom. This you know, those who love animals. And so you be in silence, as you imagine they're pointing their great massive heads towards you in holy union, in a triad of healing, and they're emitting the whale song in the sonar…singing you a lullaby of healing.

And you simply allow yourself to receive. Allowing yourself to receive, you can feel your pineal becoming cleaner and more clear. The cones and rods within the pineal begin to be able to vibrate easily. The fluid becomes purified by the power of not only the sonar, but the love that these beings have for all humanity.

For it is known that whales, dolphins, and porpoises are the guardians of humanity. They reflect the conditions of humanity. They are offering you this gift, as directed by Divine Guidance. They are offering you, Beloved, this gift of healing, receive…. receive. And now the whale song softly drifts to silence.

And you ask your new whale friends, "Oh, what can I do for you?" Pay attention to whatever sensation comes back to you. They may simply say, "Love me."

They may say, "Serve others as I have served you." They may say, "Help clean my waters." **You may simply feel the wave of love, loving you.** Aaaaahhhhh. And now, thank them… and they leave.

I will insert a personal story here. I've done some experiments with the power of divine light and live blood cells. And when I was getting lots of information from the whale kingdom, Benjamin in particular, I went to my dear friend, Dr. Patricia Felici, and I said, "I would like to do an experiment and see if the power of the whale kingdom, as I understand its divinity, would show up in my blood." Because in previous experiments, I showed the power of Divine Mother as particles of Light in my red blood cells, as viewed under a darkfield microscope. The power of Holy Spirit will change your blood and there will be sparkles of light, if you have the correct instruments to measure it.

And so, I went to my friend's laboratory, and she took a drop of my blood before I prayed... and it was normal blood, there were no sparks of light within it. Then I said a prayer, and I said, "To the kingdom of the mammals. To my great friend Benjamin. Will you send the energy of your healing love into my blood stream, into my body, and into my life?"

And I felt this beautiful tingling, healing sensation all over me. And then Patti, my dear friend, Dr. Felici took another drop of my blood, and it was filled, **filled to capacity with sparkling drops of Divine Light.**

And it was much the same shape as when I did the experiment with Divine Mother. More about that another time.

(Photo below after EFT tapping and inviting Divine Mother Light into my blood!)

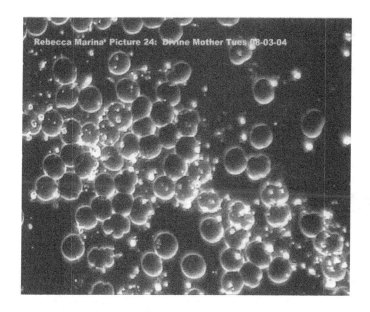

Rebecca Marina' Picture 24: Divine Mother Tues 08-03-04

To show the amazing difference of what normal blood looks like with "No Divine Light" invited — see this next photo: First Photo below, shows my blood all messed up in Roleaux formation — I applied some EFT tapping and presto! Fixed!

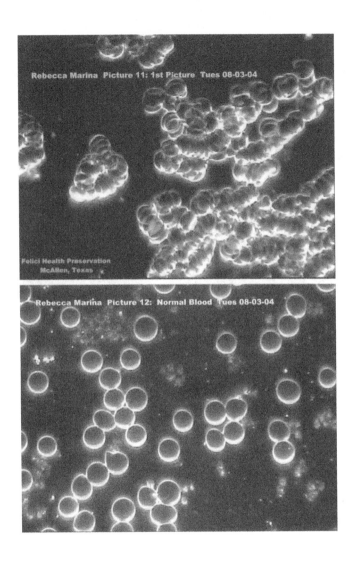

Rebecca Marina Picture 11: 1st Picture Tues 08-03-04

Felici Health Preservation
McAllen, Texas

Rebecca Marina Picture 12: Normal Blood Tues 08-03-04

Want the full story? http://wp.me/pq2xG — dK on my site.

Let us continue with the healing of the pineal. Remain in a state of meditation and feeling glowing and divine and loved. Send another wave of light out to our whale friends.

And now realizing that the pineal really goes to work when it's in darkness. That's when it secretes all the wonderful juices. That's why, when you're doing a meditation, you usually close your eyes.

Close your eyes. Just imagine that a divine hand is now closing your third eye. And close your other two eyes.

And imagine that the pineal now requests the darkness of the void because it has been stimulated, it has been cleansed. It is clean inside and outside.

Let us leave this holy divine rain within our mid-brain and this holy divine spinal column fluid with the power of the elements within our mid-brain. Let us leave it there, as we in the darkness allow even more debris to simply be carried away, dissolved by the power of this fluid.

And now knowing that your pineal gland is ready to go to work for you, you are in the power of the darkness of the void. Everything is still, and it's time to create your own miracle. To do this, drop to your heart. For the heart is where your true desires are.

And imagine that you bring the essence of your heart into the pineal. And the essence of your heart enjoys this bathing in the holy waters that are in the mid-brain. And yes, it's dark. Yes, your heart enjoys the healing darkness.

31

Now call forth the desire of your heart that you desire most to present itself to the creative powers of the pineal, to the astral plane that you have created within your mid-brain.

Speak with your mid-brain of that thing that you desire, that miracle that you want to manifest and that you want to manifest within a very short period of time. Let it be something that your heart desires, Beloved, not just something wild just from your imagination. Because the desires of your heart are part of your blueprint. The desires of your heart are those things which move you further along the evolutionary path, and the desires of your heart are the only things that truly make you happy.

So bring it out into this great darkness, into this creative void. Bring it out. And now, one tiny beam of light begins to shine upon the desire of your heart, and you see yourself having it, loving it. You are so proud of it. If you feel any shame for wanting this… take some of that holy water and wash away that shame.

Be proud that you have this desire and that you want it. Ask your angels for help in receiving this. Be open to every particle of Divine Guidance to help you receive this thing that your heart desires.

Feel the fluid within your mid-brain beginning to bubble about…and, bubbles of joy, as you see this thing materializing. Materializing into solid form and it feels as if you've <u>always</u> had it. <u>Of course</u>, you should have it. Enjoy the creation of this miracle.

Now we want to bring back in the light from your crown. Breathe in Divine Holy Spirit Light throughout all the neocortex, all the mid-brain.

Awaken the pineal. Awaken the hypothalamus, the pituitary, the brain stem, spinal column fluid. Go about your day, filled with the power of Holy Spirit Light. I love the Arabic chant meaning God's Light. An-Nūr.... An-Nūr.... An-Nūr.... An-Nūr.... An-Nūr. Fill me with light.... Fill me with light.... Fill me with light.... Fill me with light.

Take a deep breath in. Bring yourself back. In a moment, we'll take a short break, and then I will come back with a quickie version that you can do daily to keep yourself squeaky clean.

Feel free to share this gift with everyone you know who wants to discover how to cleanse the mid-brain, decalcify the pineal gland, and move into the astral plane, the plane of creation any time they desire.

My thanks go out to all the beams of light who assisted, all the ancestors.

And what's coming up as far as classes? There's a new service I've been asked to provide by my guru in the astral plane, Sri Yukteswar, which is the Bestowing of Spiritual Gifts, the Awakening of Them, and giving you the exercise to grow it... Announcement of that will come up.

A Four-Week course on mediumship, Missionary to the Other Side, will be coming up, and another course for women only, The Completely Sensual Woman will be coming up.

Many more presentations are also coming up. Let me know what you'd like to hear. If you're watching this on video, subscribe to my channel. If you are listening by audio, feel free to share that.

This is Rebecca Marina Messenger, RebeccaMarina.com.

I love you. This is the best gift I could ever give you and the best gift the Divine gave to me.

To get Your FREE Audio version of this Method, visit http://wp.me/Pq2xG — 2FR.

Quickie Version to Keep Your Pineal Clean!

Rebecca: Ready to begin with the quickie version. This will not take long. I hope you did my long version of the decalcification of the pineal gland. It did take about an hour, but hey, you're doing years' worth of work; and I did want to add, there are some dietary changes that are important, that can help.

I wanted to give you something you could do metaphysically in the astral plane to begin to decalcify and cleanse it right now. Dietary changes, of course, all the stuff we know about.

Don't eat white sugar.

Don't eat white flour.

It's not good for you, no matter what. Especially be careful with fluoride.

And a supplement that you can add, according to David Wilcox, (He wrote a book about the force fields.) — skate-fish oil, fermented skate-fish oil. Let me tell you, it stinks, but I put it in the refrigerator, and then it doesn't smell so bad when you take it. It starts to help with the cleanup process.

So, do my instant thing first, and then take the fermented skate-fish oil if you decide it. Also Spirit is telling me spirulina is very good for that.

So, they're now discovering that fluoride, which seems to be drawn to the pineal like a magnet, is also found in the thyroid. Excess fluoride is causing the thyroid to be sluggish, which can make you fat — so you don't want that.

Let me get to the quickie version. That's why you're here. So, you've done the long version. So, things you can do every day. You can do this in less than five minutes.

Begin:

Tune your awareness to the ocean, and send blessings, and ask for assistance from the whales, porpoises, and dolphins. Ask them to send their sonar waves to your mid-brain, to your pineal. They will do it.

Learn to live in that astral plane area within your mid-brain. That's where the miracles occur. And then chant the chant from Atlantis, Nome, N-O-M-E. Chant this 18 times, and then bring in light for the pineal, through the third eye, and bathe your pineal with solar light.

This is very good. It's very beneficial to be outside early in the morning. However; even late at night, you can command solar light — yes, at midnight, Beloved. Use your spiritual authority and your imagination.

Then at night, honor the darkness of the void. Honor that the pineal gland goes to work when you close your eyes. And what's really good is to bring the miracle that you want into your pineal gland when you go into sleep.

Bring that miracle there, and begin to enjoy it in the astral plane, where everything is created instantly. You have your own astral plane within the mid-brain. Start taking advantage of it. Enjoy it.

This is the quickie version. This is Rebecca Marina Messenger. You can visit me at RebeccaMarina.com.

Subscribe to this channel, if you're watching this on video, and you'll get all kinds of presentations. It's my joy to be a Light Worker and a servant of the Divine, and I have loved sharing this quickie version with you. So, thank you so much.

To get Your FREE Audio version of this Method, visit http://wp.me/Pq2xG — 2FR.

37

Appendix

Basic Heart Point Technique (HPT)

(Get the entire Heart Point Technique manual, including detailed images FREE at RebeccaMarina.com.)

Description

HPT is a healing method sent from the Divine Feminine. HPT accesses the deepest wisdom of the heart and teaches soul mastery. HPT flows light energy through various acupressure meridians, organs, and glands. HPT is a spiritual/energetic healing modality.

Treatment with HPT consists of "running light" through treatment points beginning with:

- **Higher Self point** (18-24 inches above head)

- **Crown point** (through corpus callosum, pineal gland, hypothalamus)

- **Third eye**, **beginning of eyebrow**, **side of eye**, **2 points just above the tear duct** and **under eye** [These are the points your hand is covering: third eye (inner vision), beginning of eyebrow (sadness), side of eye (anger), under eye (fear), inside corner of eye 1/8 inch above tear duct (site where all acupressure points enter the brain).]

- **Heart point** (just to left of center of chest)
- **Consolidation point** at nape of neck (this is used AFTER intensity is lowered) to 'tap in' a positive keyword

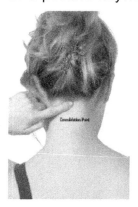

Consolidation Point

Step 1. Set intention of what to work on (make sure client understands all the treatment points).

Step 2. Get an intensity rating–if this applies– from 1 to 10 (1 is low; 10 is high). As the practitioner, write down this number, as well as the condition or emotion.

Step 3. If this is an emotion, ask where they feel it in their body. Ask: if this emotion had a voice, what kind of energy would it need to feel better?

Step 4. Simply accept the emotion or condition without judgment. Hold it up the light for healing as you begin to run light through the HPT points.

Step 5. Put your awareness on the higher-self point, call in light, imagine the light overflowing down into the crown, through all the points and resting in the wisdom of the heart.

If a certain energy was requested to make it feel better, interchange that name with the ancient Arabic phrase 'An-Nūr,' (pronounced Ahn Noor) e.g. if client said the energy of 'acceptance' was needed, use 'An-Nūr' and 'acceptance' alternately. This is optional.

Because An-Nūr is incorruptible and

self-adjusting, it can be used alone or
with other words.

Tell your client to relax and simply pay
attention to what comes up.

Step 6. Chant 'An-Nūr' on behalf of your client.
It is good if they chant with you. I
usually start with 27 times, but you will
'get' a number in your head. It can be
less or more but should be at least 7
times.

Step 7. Check back in with client and ask them
to take another intensity rating
between 1 and 10. It should have gone
down. Sometimes, it changes to a
different emotion or condition.

Proceed to work on that one emotion
the same way. The key here is to
simply accept whatever comes up and
send light, mercy, and the chant to
that... no judgment.

HPT Points

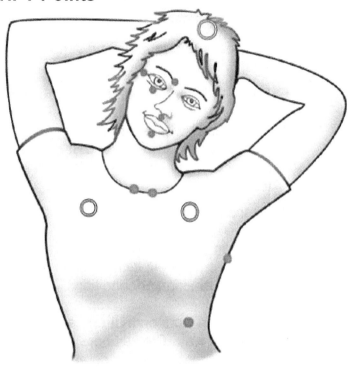

HPT Tapping

In some cases, action is required. You can tap on the HPT points, repeating the issues.

For instance, if you feel angry, tap the HPT points, simply stating the emotion you feel.

First, tune into the emotion holding HPT and get an intensity rating on a scale of 1-10.

Tapping at the crown: "I feel angry."

Third eye: "I feel angry."

Beginning of eye: "I feel angry."

Side of the eye: "I feel angry."

Under the eye: "I feel angry."

Inner eye points: "I feel angry."

Heart point: "I feel angry,"

Feel free to add any other words that express your anger, e.g. "That rotten scalawag makes me so angry!" It really helps to intensify the release, if you allow yourself to fully get into the emotions of a little child when expressing any deep emotion.

When the intensity is way down, tap in a positive keyword (how do you want to feel instead?) at the consolidation point at the back of the head.

Additions to Make HPT Even More Effective

Pranic tube breathing: the pranic tube runs from the perineum up to the top of the head. Breathing this way causes balance to be restored.

The Pranic Tube

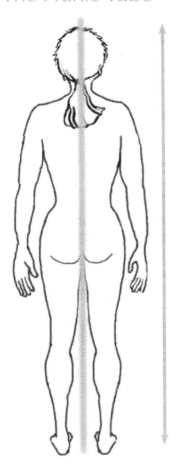

How to do Pranic Tube Breathing: Imagine you are breathing the energies of the earth up through the perineum and into the heart center. Imagine breathing the energies of the heavens down from the crown and into the heart. Realize this energy is always flowing.

Sound: Make the sound of the emotion. According to The Hathors (advanced beings channeled by Tom Kenyon) every emotion has a sound signature. By getting in touch with the emotion–allowing whatever primal sound we could imagine to come out–we allow it to be transmuted.

Sacred Arabic Chants: Chanting these phrases into the emotion/condition brings relief and healing. (An-Nūr is an example.)

Movement: If the emotion could move, what kind of movement would it be?

Helpful to ask: (holding HPT points) What kind of energy is needed to heal this?

Coming Soon by Rebecca Marina Messenger

Jesus was Not Born Magic: How He Learned to Do His Miracles, and How You Can Too!

Made in the USA
Monee, IL
12 May 2022